I0420838

Quote Octopus
Melbourne, Victoria, 3053
Australia
www.quoteoctopus.com

The name Muhammad is the most common name in the world. In all the countries around the world - Pakistan, Saudi Arabia, Morocco, Turkey, Syria, Lebanon - there are more Muhammads than anything else. When I joined the Nation of Islam and became a Muslim, they gave me the most famous name because I was the champ.

**Muhammad Ali**


When the Industrial Revolution started, the amount of carbon sitting underneath Britain in the form of coal was as big as the amount of carbon sitting under Saudi Arabia in the form of oil, and this carbon powered the Industrial Revolution, it put the 'Great' in Great Britain, and led to Britain's temporary world domination.

**David J. C. MacKay**


One of the most extreme dictatorships, and the most important one from the U.S. point of view, is Saudi Arabia. Saudi Arabia is the most extreme fundamentalist state in the world. It's also a missionary state. It's expending huge efforts - has been for many years - to disseminate its extremist Wahhabi-Salafi version of Islam, all with U.S. backing.

**Noam Chomsky**


You know, Saudi Arabia has a lot of poverty also. Regardless about what you hear about the viceroy and people being rich, et cetera.

**Al-Waleed bin Talal**

Too many countries that do not play by the free trade rules of the World Trade Organization - including, notably mercantilist China and monopolist Saudi Arabia - have been allowed in, to the detriment of both the WTO and the liberal trading environment it is supposed to sponsor.

**Frank Gaffney**

The rise to prominence of the Saudi novel in Arabic is the great man-bites-dog of recent world literature. Saudi Arabia is a country without a free press, where European styles and forms are distrusted and where the female half of the population became literate only in this generation.

**James Buchan**

The Saudi government's denial of basic rights to women is not only wrong, it hurts Saudi Arabia's economic development, modernization and prosperity.

**Barbara Boxer**

To allow the construction of places of worship other than Islamic ones in Saudi Arabia, it would be like asking the Vatican to build a mosque inside of it.

**Abdullah of Saudi Arabia**

I saw a report yesterday. There's so much oil, all over the world, they don't know where to dump it. And Saudi Arabia says, 'Oh, there's too much oil.' They - they came back yesterday. Did you see the report? They want to reduce oil production. Do you think they're our friends? They're not our friends.

**Donald Trump**

My mother might find a thin gold chain at the back of a drawer, wadded into an impossibly tight knot, and give it to me to untangle. It would have a shiny, sweaty smell, and excite me: Gold chains linked you to the great fairy tales and myths, to Arabia, and India; to the great weight of the world, but lighter than a feather.

**Anne Lamott**

I met a lot of great people in Saudi Arabia and I'd like to see them again. And I'd love to spend more time in the desert and in the mountains. I felt really at home there.

**Dave Eggers**

I would like to find a way in which people in Saudi Arabia could learn that they can be something other than a Muslim. Some people may not realize this. Of course, there is the problem that you can get in trouble or get stoned.

**Richard Dawkins**

If Iran and North Korea, by some horrible, devilish, nightmarish scenario, got together and went to war at the same time, one against Saudi Arabia and one against South Korea, I don't know what we would do about that. I don't know that we could stop them short of using nuclear weapons.

**Ben Stein**

Saudi Arabia has also changed. People today are connecting with each other all across the world through small gadgets and television. It's a different society.

**Sultan bin Abdul-Aziz Al Saud**

Islam is unusual in that it's the only one of the great world religions which was born inside recorded history. That there's an enormous amount of factual historical record about the life of a prophet and about social conditions in Arabia at that time. So it's possible to look at the origin of Islam in a scholarly way.

**Salman Rushdie**

The mistake of the West was to put the Sauds on the throne of Saudi Arabia and give them control of the world's oil fortune, which they then used to propagate Wahhabi Islam.

**Salman Rushdie**

Saudi Arabia operates according to the belief that God made young men and women so utterly and completely without self-control that they must be physically segregated every moment of the day and night.

**James Buchan**

The corporate right fires up the religious right against gay marriage and abortion and uses their votes to push their deregulation and tax cuts for the rich. It's an old trick. The House of Saud has the same arrangement with the Mullahs in Saudi Arabia.

**Adam McKay**

Other places are also generators of far-flung violence beyond their own borders - Pakistan and Saudi Arabia are obvious examples - but none has as long a history of war, resistance, and terror as Chechnya.

**Stephen Kinzer**

The funny thing is that I'm the girl who no one sees at the beach. Ask anyone who's traveled with me. Normally, I'm in so many layers, I look like Lawrence of Arabia!

**Vera Wang**

Saudi Arabia is a puritanical state that claims a monopoly of wisdom and virtue.

**James Buchan**


I mean, it was a mummy movie. It was a good film independent of its source. It that looks like Lawrence of Arabia on steroids in a lot of ways.

**Brendan Fraser**


Most of the suicide hijackers came from Saudi Arabia, a place not lacking in wealth. But due to rapid population growth, the wealth per capita has fallen by about half in a generation.

**Keith Henson**


Street protests in Saudi Arabia might warm our hearts, but they could easily lead to $250 a barrel oil and a global recession.

**Fareed Zakaria**


I'm telling you, you can't compare Saudi Arabia to other countries.

**Al-Waleed bin Talal**


I never met Peter O'Toole, but he one was of those rare actors whose success was defined by a single role. His incandescent performance in David Lean's 'Lawrence of Arabia' is one that nobody who saw it will ever forget.

**Michael Korda**


The notion that a contemporary woman must look mannish in order to be taken seriously as a seeker of power is frankly dismaying. This is America, not Saudi Arabia.

**Anna Wintour**


Actually, King Abdullah, under his supervision and guidance, has established a dialogue in Saudi Arabia whereby all the population, whether Shiite or Sunnis from north, south, west or east, they can get together and exchange their views.

**Al-Waleed bin Talal**


There's no question that tar sands in Canada are probably the largest source of oil available to the U.S. over a long period of time. There's as much oil in the tar sands probably as there is in Saudi Arabia. The problem is, there's a huge capital requirement to develop that.

**T. Boone Pickens**


Some have said it is the easiest group at the World Cup, but we realize it won't be like that. Germany are a tremendous side, but to be honest I don't know much about Cameroon and Saudi Arabia.

**Robbie Keane**

It is no secret that many Islamic movements in the Middle East tend to be authoritarian, and some of the so-called 'Islamic regimes' such as Saudi Arabia, Iran - and the worst case was the Taliban in Afghanistan - they are pretty authoritarian. No doubt about that.

**Mustafa Akyol**

Look, I don't think President Obama would have bowed to the ruler of Saudi Arabia if he didn't have oil to the degree that the Saudis do. I think they and other producing states, almost all of whom, except Norway and Canada, are dictatorships or autocratic systems, have thrown their weight around because of oil.

**James Woolsey**

So, I think even in Saudi Arabia there is movement. And we have to remember that over the years they've stabilized the oil price and that is tremendously important for the economies of the world. I think we have no choice but to work with the government of Saudi Arabia.

**Frank Carlucci**

Additionally, any Human Rights Council reform that allows countries with despicable human rights records to remain as members, such as China and Saudi Arabia, is not real reform.

**Michael McCaul**


Saud bin Abd al-Aziz was the moon-faced, shortsighted, bespectacled son of the old founder of Saudi Arabia, who'd always been his father's protege but had never quite lived up to everything that his father had.

**Robert Lacey**


Our relations with brothers in Gulf Cooperation council are good and developing, either bilateral relations or with the G.C.C itself, also we have good brotherly and solid ties with Saudi Arabia.

**Ali Abdullah Saleh**


If Iran obtains nuclear weapons, then almost certainly Saudi Arabia will do the same, as will Egypt, Turkey and perhaps others in the region.

**John Bolton**


Most dramatically, and perhaps least noticed, is the violence inside Saudi Arabia itself.

**Michael Scheuer**

The Kingdom of Saudi Arabia, like other countries in the region, rejects the acquisition of nuclear weapons by anyone, especially nuclear weapons in the Middle East region. We hope that such weapons will be banned or eliminated from the region by every country in the region.

**Abdullah of Saudi Arabia**

Even non-democratic allies no longer trust America. Barack Obama has alienated our most important and longest standing Arab allies, Egypt and Saudi Arabia. Both the anti-Muslim Brotherhood and the anti-Iran Arab states have lost respect for him.

**Dennis Prager**

The anchors of the Arab consensus have long been Egypt and Saudi Arabia, and both are now weakened forces in Arab politics and diplomacy.

**Elliott Abrams**

America is the Saudi Arabia of coal.

**Charles Duhigg**

Traditionally, all the kings of Saudi Arabia have been sons of the founder of Saudi Arabia, and they've gone from one son to the next.

**Richard Engel**


If I were a child of Tibet or of Arabia, I suspect the path I'd walk would be the Buddhist path or the Muslim path. And I don't mind saying that I don't invalidate any of those paths.

**John Shelby Spong**


In some countries that are darlings of the West, like Egypt, everyone knows the result of national elections years in advance: The man in power always wins. In others, like Saudi Arabia, the very idea of an election is unthinkable.

**Stephen Kinzer**


But Saudi Arabia is surprising in a lot of ways. Like any place, or any people, it relentlessly defies easy categorization.

**Dave Eggers**


It is in Saudi Arabia's best interest to allow women to fully participate in its society, and this includes the right to vote and run for office.

**Barbara Boxer**

I've always loved the old epics that tell a simple emotional story, whether it's the tumultuous relationship between Rhett and Scarlett or Lawrence of Arabia's passion to get lost in a faraway place.

**Baz Luhrmann**


Lebanon is restless, Syria got its walking papers, Egypt is scheduling elections with more than one candidate, and even Saudi Arabia, whose rulers are perhaps more terrified of women than rulers anywhere else in the world, allowed limited municipal elections.

**Suzanne Fields**


I have never connected with 'Gone With the Wind.' 'Lawrence of Arabia' leaves me cold.

**Stephen Hunter**


Saudi Arabia has stability. The social contract and the political contract between the king and the rulers and the royal family and the ruled people in Saudi Arabia is very strong and the bondage is so solid.

**Al-Waleed bin Talal**

As far as Iraq, the important thing is that the Taliban is gone in Afghanistan, three-quarters of the al-Qaida leadership is either dead or in jail, and we now have Saudi Arabia working with us, Pakistan working with us.

**Peter T. King**


And in Iraq we tried to implement the same policy that was so successful in Saudi Arabia, but Saddam Hussein didn't buy. When the economic hit men fail in this scenario, the next step is what we call the jackals.

**John Perkins**


I should like to repeat what I stated recently in the Jeddah Economic Forum in Saudi Arabia: It won't be the religion, but rather the world-view of some of its followers that shall be made current.

**Recep Tayyip Erdogan**


The Taliban, broadly speaking, are Afghans - farmers, subsistence farmers. As I say, most of those people can't find the United States on the map. Al Qaeda, traditionally, are much more educated, middle-class people, often from Egypt, from Saudi Arabia, North Africa.

**Rory Stewart**

We are living in a different world now. You can see it everywhere in international relations: It was noteworthy that, after his visit to Washington, the Chinese president's next stop was Saudi Arabia.

**Daniel Yergin**

Some countries, like Saudi Arabia, where the population growth is very high, whereby you don't have the mortgage low yet. Still the demand outstrips supply by much.

**Al-Waleed bin Talal**

The bulk of extra supplies that could be put into the market come from two places. One, they come from other Persian Gulf suppliers, of which Saudi Arabia is at the top of the list.

**Daniel Yergin**

My own center, my Kingdom Center, which is the highest priced tower in Saudi Arabia, was vacated twice because of terrorist attacks, terrorist threats.

**Al-Waleed bin Talal**

I move countries every three or four years. I was born in London, and we lived in Canada. Then we lived in Saudi Arabia until the Gulf War broke out, when we were forced to leave. Then we hop-scotched for a while from Holland back to

Canada back to Saudi Arabia. Then there was D-day, so we had to get out again.

**Hannah Simone**


I understand the Saudis have been named because fifteen of the nineteen hijackers were from Saudi Arabia.

**Sibel Edmonds**


India considers Saudi Arabia a center of stability in the region. The security and stability of the Gulf region and that of the Indian subcontinent are interlinked. Bilateral security cooperation between India and Saudi Arabia will contribute to regional stability and in addressing the common threat of terrorism in the region.

**Salman Khurshid**


But the key thing is that Iraq, while it's got very large oil reserves, has marginalized itself as an oil exporter and these days its exports are only about one tenth that of neighboring Saudi Arabia.

**Daniel Yergin**


If China was like the moon, then arriving in Saudi Arabia was Mars. At least you can see the moon from Earth.

**Basmah bint Saud**

The way women today are treated in Saudi Arabia is a direct result of the education our children, boys and girls, receive at school.

**Basmah bint Saud**


I covered the first Gulf War in Saudi Arabia and Israel for ABC News.

**Leslie Cockburn**


If you compare the size of our reserves of Saudi Arabia and the whole Middle East, it's like three times as much as all of that combined and that's just the easily, readily available 1800 billion barrels and there are probably 3 billion barrels that are commercially just under that, available.

**Chris Cannon**


I lived in Saudi Arabia in the late 1970s. It was, for a Westerner, pretty idyllic. There were the religious police; there were the rules; there were the prayer times. But it was as if we were existing in two separate universes. The Westerners were just allowed to get on with their way of life.

**Robert Lacey**

Well, the first thing I wanted to be was a carpenter. Then I wanted to be a painter and then a singer. It was when I first saw 'Lawrence of Arabia' that I wanted to be an actor.

**Michael Pitt**


There are different opinions across the Middle East of Al-Jazeera. They've been kicked out of Egypt and Jordan and then let back in; they've been totally banned from Saudi Arabia, Sudan and Syria.

**Jehane Noujaim**


I went to Saudi Arabia in 2010, and spent most of my time in Jeddah and the King Abdullah Economic City.

**Dave Eggers**


Saudi Arabia is one of India's most valued strategic partners.

**Salman Khurshid**


For 22 years, Bandar bin Sultan was Saudi Arabia's influential, irrepressible ambassador in Washington.

**Elliott Abrams**


Saudi Arabia has allowed training on its soil of American forces.

**Joe Biden**

Over the years, I've spent time in Saudi Arabia, the Bekaa Valley, Afghanistan, Jordan, and Kenya, among other vacation hotspots.

**Alex Berenson**

Saudi Arabia supplies much oil to the U.S. And it is the world's largest consumer of American weaponry.

**Stephen Kinzer**

The idea that Arabia is best run by Arabs is no more palatable to Western leaders today than it was to Napoleon or Churchill.

**Stephen Kinzer**

Weapons systems the U.S. sold to the Shah of Iran wound up in the hands of Islamic militants who seized power there in 1979; a comparable scenario in Saudi Arabia is hardly impossible.

**Stephen Kinzer**

The Syrian border town of Qa'im was the main gateway Islamic radicals used to go to Iraq. Syria became the passageway for extremists from Egypt, Libya, Afghanistan,

Yemen, Saudi Arabia and other Muslim nations to fight a jihad against American forces in Iraq.

**Richard Engel**


There are companies trying to build business within Saudi Arabia, and what they find is that if they try to bring on locals and teach them how to become senior executives, they just don't show up to work. They are not predictable as to when they'll come in and how much of their hearts are into that opportunity.

**Clayton Christensen**


I grew up in Somalia, in Saudi Arabia, in Ethiopia, and in Kenya. I came to Europe in 1992, when I was 22, and became a member of Parliament in Holland.

**Ayaan Hirsi Ali**


Lawrence of Arabia is the ultimate movie, deeply cinematic.

**Christine Baranski**


You know, in Saudi Arabia, there is a body of 40 people - 34 people exactly, that once the succession comes, they will meet and they will elect a king in there.

**Al-Waleed bin Talal**

Saudi Arabia was, until just a few years ago, probably one of the most safe countries on earth. And now the paper is daily full of activities and shootouts between Islamists who supported Osama bin Laden and the government there.

**Michael Scheuer**


The Crown Prince has said he needs to broaden political participation in the governing of Saudi Arabia.

**Frank Carlucci**


The first concert that my parents took me to was in this canyon in Saudi Arabia called Buttermilk Canyon. You sleep under the stars in the desert, and ex-pats - German, Swiss, Canadian, American - would play classical music that filled the whole canyon.

**Hannah Simone**


Losing their reproductive rights is the first step to how women live in Saudi Arabia and Afghanistan.

**Patricia Richardson**


'Lawrence of Arabia' is a film that anyone wanting to become an actor should watch at least six hundred times.

**Sid Haig**

We have to fight radical Islam wherever it exists. It's in Afghanistan, it's in Saudi Arabia, throughout the Middle-East in big numbers and it's in the United States.

**Tom Tancredo**

I wouldn't write anything autobiographical. If you've lived a life like Laurence of Arabia, it might be a consideration, but otherwise it's a little bit vain, it seems to me.

**James Lee Burke**

On the whole, it is the rights and freedoms of all citizens that are crucial in Saudi Arabia and from those the rights of women will emanate.

**Basmah bint Saud**

I'm not sure where I'm from! I was born in London. My father's from Ghana but lives in Saudi Arabia. My mother's Nigerian but lives in Ghana. I grew up in Boston.

**Taiye Selasi**

I think the real target of al-Qaeda is Saudi Arabia by the way. They hate us and we're a vehicle to get at Saudi Arabia. I think

Osama bin Laden really wants to topple that regime and have his people move in, but that's a whole other story.

**Frank Carlucci**


The Treasury Department would use the interest from these securities to hire U.S. companies to build Saudi Arabia - new cities, new infrastructure - which we've done.

**John Perkins**


I love to look at The Graduate, or Lawrence of Arabia, or things I had nothing to do with. But you could not get me to go back and watch movies that it was a privilege just to be around them when they were being made.

**Jeffrey Katzenberg**


I want to state clearly that I am a humanitarian, not an activist. I do not follow any agendas - only that of humanity, not only in Saudi Arabia, but all over the world.

**Basmah bint Saud**


Like Afghanistan before it, Iraq is only one theater in a regional war. We were attacked by a network of terrorist organizations supported by several countries, of whom the most important were Iran, Iraq, Syria, and Saudi Arabia.

**Michael Ledeen**

Very few people are fortunate enough to walk through countries like Iran, Iraq, Syria, Lebanon, Jordan, and Saudi Arabia, and I had seen them all. I had spoken to many on the street.

**Ashleigh Banfield**


I would love to live stream them all, so if you're in New York and you come along, you can watch Tropfest N.Y., and six weeks later you are watching Tropfest Arabia or Tropfest Australia live stream, and so they are all connected.

**John Polson**

www.ingramcontent.com/pod-product-compliance
Lightning Source LLC
Chambersburg PA
CBHW072024290526
45787CB00014B/1866